CONTENTS

Weapons Under the Water

Hundreds of feet (m) below the ocean surface, a long, black shape pushes through the water. A **submarine** is hiding from a ship above. The submarine plays a game of hide and seek with the ship, and the submarine easily wins. The submarine moves away without the ship ever knowing it was there.

Submarines are the U.S. Navy's most powerful **weapons**. Submarines can strike the enemy anytime and anywhere. They can hit an enemy at sea from hundreds of miles (km) away. With submarines hiding below, the enemy will not know where to hit back.

Amazing
Military
Vehicles

NAVY SUBMARINES
IN ACTION

Kay Jackson

PowerKiDS press™

New York

For Doug—Explore. Dream. Discover.

Published in 2009 by The Rosen Publishing Group, Inc.
29 East 21st Street, New York, NY 10010

First Edition

Editor: Nicole Pristash
Book Design: Julio Gil
Photo Researcher: Jessica Gerweck

Photo Credits: Cover © U.S. Navy/Age Fotostock; pp. 5, 9, 10, 13, 17, 18, 21 U.S. Navy Photo; pp. 6, 17 (inset) © Getty Images; p. 14 © Steve Kaufman/Age Fotostock.

Library of Congress Cataloging-in-Publication Data

Jackson, Kay, 1959–
   Navy submarines in action / Kay Jackson. — 1st ed.
      p. cm. — (Amazing military vehicles)
   Includes index.
   ISBN 978-1-4358-2751-6 (library binding) — ISBN 978-1-4358-3161-2 (pbk.)
ISBN 978-1-4358-3167-4 (6-pack)
   1. Submarines (Ships—United States—Juvenile literature. 2. United States. Navy—Juvenile literature. I. Title.
   V858.J33 2009
   623.825'7—dc22
                                        2008035275

Manufactured in the United States of America

CPSIA Compliance Information: Batch #211370PK: For Further Information Contact Rosen Publishing, New York, New York at 1-800-237-9932

Submarines are long and tube shaped. These crew members are standing on the sail of the submarine, which sticks out from the top.

This is a drawing of the submarine *Hunley*. In 1864, during the Civil War, the *Hunley* became the first submarine to sink an enemy warship.

Pig Boats

Submarines became a part of American history during the American Revolution. In 1776, a small, wooden submarine named *Turtle* tried to attack a British ship in New York City's harbor. It was not until 1862, though, that submarines became a part of the U.S. Navy. These first Navy submarines were so hot and dirty inside that they were nicknamed pig boats.

Submarines have changed a lot since then. Today, submarines are cool, clean, and comfortable. They carry dozens of **torpedoes** and **missiles** that help keep people safe. A submarine is designed, or made, to carry out the Navy's important jobs.

How Submarines Submerge

A submarine uses water and air to help it **submerge** and then surface. To sink, a submarine fills its **tanks** with water. U.S. Navy submarines can sink deeper than 800 feet (244 m). To rise, the submarine uses air. First, air blows the water out of the tanks. Then, the tanks fill up with air.

Modern submarines have smooth **hulls** that are shaped like teardrops. The hulls are painted black to help the submarine hide from the enemy. All Navy submarines use **nuclear energy**, which allows submarines to stay underwater for a very long time.

When submarines do not need to hide underwater, they can move on the surface of the water, like the submarine shown here.

Here the USS *Hampton* (front), a submarine, is shown traveling with the USS *Chafee* (left) and the USS *Kitty Hawk* (right) after a training exercise.

Defend and Attack

The Navy has bases on land, as other branches of the U.S. military do. However, the Navy does most of its work at sea. The Navy uses large, powerful ships, but submarines are some of the Navy's most important tools.

Navy submarines have two jobs, to **defend** and to attack. Submarines often travel with large groups of ships. They help defend the groups against enemy ships and submarines. If an enemy ship gets too close, submarines will attack by firing missiles. Submarines also fire missiles at enemy bridges, factories, and airfields. Submarines can spot the enemy from very far away.

Sonar and Periscopes

Submarines stay underwater much of the time. To know what is around them, submarines use **sonar**. Sonar picks up sounds coming from ships and other submarines. Sonar can even pick up the sounds of whales and other animals!

To see what is above the surface of the water, a submarine crew uses a periscope, which sticks out above the water. A periscope is a long tube that allows a picture to be seen through it. Modern submarines have periscopes that can take pictures of what is around them. These periscopes can also zoom in on objects and see at night.

A periscope is an important tool for a submarine crew. In this picture, a woman is learning how to use a periscope aboard the USS *Alaska*.

This is a control room on a Navy submarine. The control room houses a submarine's controls, periscopes, and GPS.

Running a Submarine

Today's Navy submarines are powered by nuclear energy, which heats water into steam. The steam turns **generators** that make electricity. Steam also spins the submarine's **propeller**. The propeller's blades push the submarine through the water.

While on the surface, a submarine uses a Global Positioning System, or GPS, to find its way. A GPS is a tool that helps something find its location on a map. With a GPS, the crew can figure out where their submarine is. Then, the crew can carry out their job. The crew's job depends on what type of submarine the crew is on.

Boomers

Ballistic submarines are submarines that are made to fire ballistic missiles. Ballistic missiles are guided in the air at first, but then they fall freely toward the ground later. A ballistic submarine is 560 feet (171 m) long, and it carries around 24 ballistic missiles. Ballistic submarines are often called boomers because of their many powerful weapons.

While on jobs, ballistic submarines will hide for months under water. When the U.S. Navy wants to show its power, though, it sends a ballistic submarine to troubled places in the world. Then, the boomer will surface in view of its enemies.

The USS *Pennsylvania*, a ballistic submarine, is shown here. *Inset*: Here you can see a Trident II ballistic missile being fired from a submarine.

Here the USS *Miami*, an attack submarine, is shown surfacing in the North Arabian Sea. Attack submarines are fast, making them hard for enemies to find.

Small but Fast

Attack submarines are made to chase and attack enemy submarines and ships. Attack submarines are smaller and faster than ballistic submarines. Attack submarines fire torpedoes and guided missiles. A guided missile's path can be changed while it is in the air.

Attack submarines have dangerous jobs. One job is to shadow enemy submarines. An attack submarine will listen for an enemy submarine, and then it will follow the enemy carefully. Attack submarines also have small fighting teams that carry out secret jobs. First, the submarine moves close to shore. Then, the team leaves the submarine through a special opening.

Earning the Dolphins

Submarine crew members, or submariners, are some of the most highly trained people in the Navy. To become submariners, students first go to a Navy school to learn basic skills. Students also practice escaping from a sunken submarine. Then, a submariner may go on to learn a skill. He might become an electrician, a torpedo man, or a cook.

Submariners also train while they are on their submarines. Every submariner has to learn how everything on a submarine works. When the training is over, the best students earn a dolphin pin. This pin is a symbol, or sign, of Navy submarine service.

Navy submariners travel all over the world in their submarines. This crew is working in the North Pole.

Submarines of Tomorrow

The Navy believes submarines will be needed for a long time to come. The submarines of tomorrow will cost less, and they will be able to do more. For example, the Navy's latest submarines have small boats that can observe the enemy without being seen. Some new submarines do not have periscopes. Instead, special cameras provide a view of the surface.

As the Navy continues to grow and change, submarines will follow. There is a reason the Navy has used submarines for so many years. Submarines can be counted on to defend the Navy and to keep people safe.

Glossary

defend (dih-FEND) To guard from harm.

generators (JEH-neh-ray-turz) Machines that make electricity.

hulls (HULZ) The frames, or outer bodies, of ships.

missiles (MIH-sulz) Weapons that are shot at something far away.

nuclear energy (NOO-klee-ur EH-nur-jee) The power in the center of an atom, which is the smallest bit of matter.

propeller (pruh-PEL-er) A paddlelike part on an object that spins to move the object forward.

sonar (SOH-nahr) A way of using underwater sound waves to find objects or judge distances.

submarine (SUB-muh-reen) A ship that is made to travel underwater.

submerge (sub-MERJ) To put underwater.

tanks (TANGKS) Large objects for holding water or other matter.

torpedoes (tor-PEE-dohz) Underwater missiles that blow up when they hit something.

weapons (WEH-punz) Objects used to hurt or kill.

Index

Web Sites

Due to the changing nature of Internet links, PowerKids Press has developed an online list of Web sites related to the subject of this book. This site is updated regularly. Please use this link to access the list:

www.powerkidslinks.com/amv/subm/